curious about

TIGER SHARKS

BY DEBRA RANDORF

AMICUS LEARNING

What are you

curious about?

Curious About is published by
Amicus Learning, an imprint of Amicus
P.O. Box 227, Mankato, MN 56002
www.amicuspublishing.us

Editor: Ana Brauer
Series Designer: Kathleen Petelinsek
Book Designer and Photo Researcher: Sara Hood

Library of Congress Cataloging-in-Publication Data
Names: Randorf, Debra, author.
Title: Curious about tiger sharks / by Debra Randorf.
Description: Mankato, MN : Amicus Learning, [2026] | Series: Curious about sharks | Includes bibliographical references and index. | Audience: Ages 6–9 | Audience: Grades 2–3 | Summary: "Did you know tiger sharks get called the trash cans of the sea? They'll eat anything, even garbage! Learn about these fascinating sharks in this question-and-answer book for elementary-aged readers. Includes infographics, table of contents, glossary, books and websites for further research, and index"— Provided by publisher.
Identifiers: LCCN 2024048300 (print) | LCCN 2024048301 (ebook) | ISBN 9798892005074 (library binding) | ISBN 9798892005616 (paperback) | ISBN 9798892006156 (ebook)
Subjects: LCSH: Tiger shark—Juvenile literature.
Classification: LCC QL638.95.C3 R37 2026 (print) | LCC QL638.95.C3 (ebook) | DDC 597.3/4—dc23/eng/20241129
LC record available at https://lccn.loc.gov/2024048300
LC ebook record available at https://lccn.loc.gov/2024048301

Photo Credits: Alamy Stock Photo/Amanda Cotton, 6–7, Helmut Corneli, 3, 20–21, Jeff Rotman, 13, Luiz Puntel, 2, 5, WaterFrame_gno, 18–19; Blue Planet Archive/Doug Perrine, 16–17; Dreamstime/Photon75, 9; Getty Images/Gregory Sweeney, 15, Samuel J Coe, 2, 12; Shutterstock/Jsegalexplore, cover, 1, 10, Wonderful Nature, 8–9; The Noun Project/Amethyst Studio, 22, Hugo RICHIR, 23, monkik, 23, Tanapol Ngoenchairoj, 22; Vecteezy/om1947, 7

Printed in India

CHAPTER ONE

Why are they called tiger sharks?

When they are born, they have dark stripes like a tiger. That's how they got their name! The stripes fade as the shark grows. Tiger sharks are blueish gray on top and white on their belly. They also eat a lot! They are famous for their big **appetites**!

Tiger sharks are at the top of the food chain. No animal hunts them.

Can I swim with one?

No! Tiger sharks are **aggressive** animals. They are more likely to attack swimmers than other sharks. They are found in warm water all around the world. Tiger sharks are some of the most dangerous sharks in the ocean.

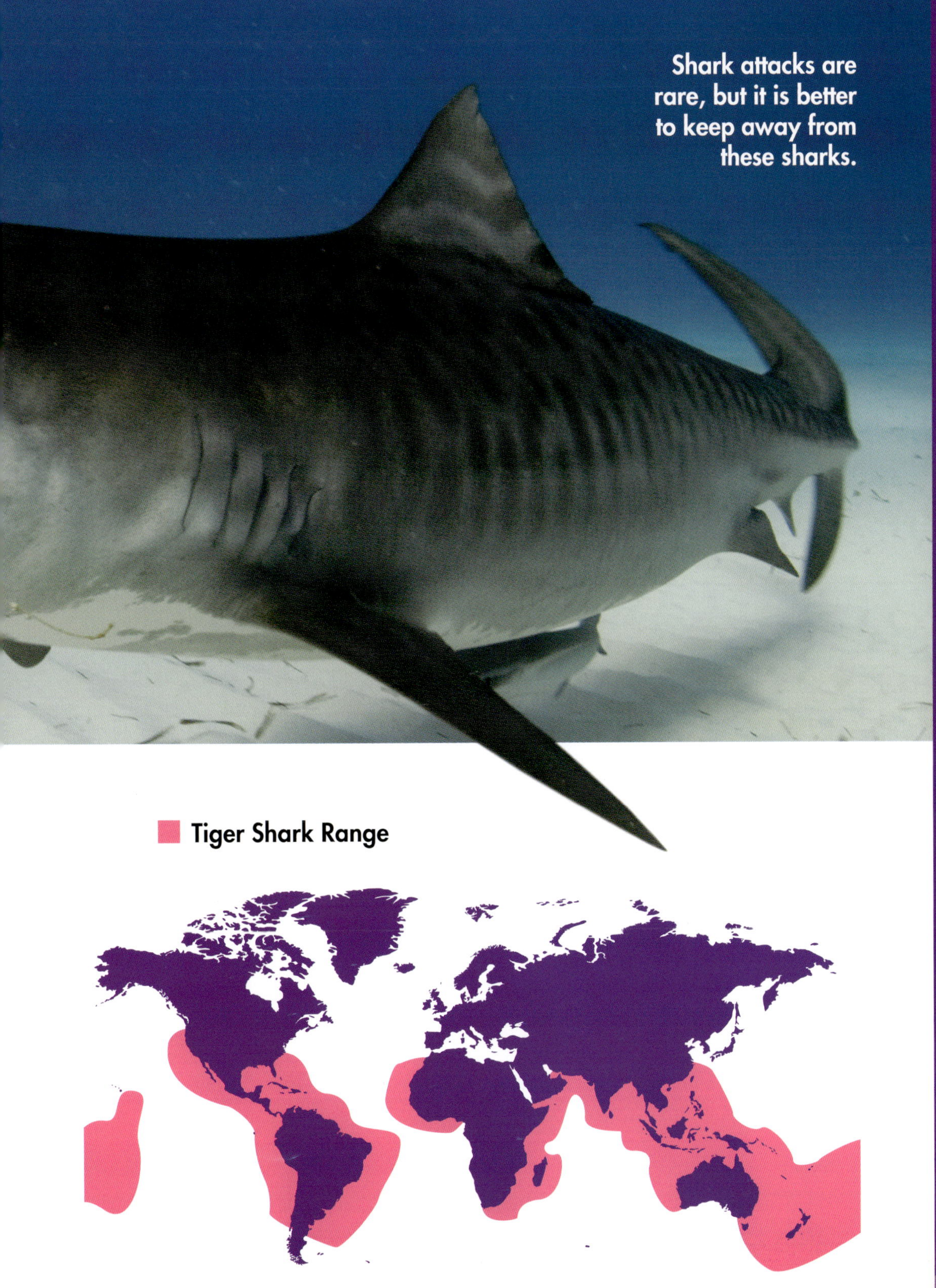
Shark attacks are rare, but it is better to keep away from these sharks.
Tiger Shark Range

Why are they so dangerous?

Tiger sharks swim close to shore. This makes them a bigger risk to people. Tiger sharks also have special teeth. Their teeth have curved, saw-like edges. This helps the sharks trap their **prey**.

This shark is likely to mistake someone for a seal and attack.

DID YOU KNOW?
The special shape of tiger shark teeth helps them crush and eat sea turtle shells.

CHAPTER TWO

What do tiger sharks eat?

Remora fish often attach themselves to a shark. They eat the scraps of the shark's meal.

Almost anything! Tiger sharks are not picky eaters. They will eat fish, sea turtles, stingrays, squid, other sharks, and even garbage. Tires, clothing, wallets, and even pieces of boats and ships have been found in tiger shark stomachs.

DID YOU KNOW?
The tiger shark is known as the "trash can of the sea."

Tiger sharks also eat dead animals.

How do tiger sharks hunt?

They usually come near the shore to hunt at night. Their prey is easier to sneak up on in the dark. The sharks return to deeper water during the day. Tiger sharks use their great eyesight and sense of smell to find food.

Tiger sharks will also hunt during the day if they are very hungry.

How fast does a tiger shark swim?

Not very fast. Tiger sharks are slow, calm swimmers. They swim at about 3 miles (4.8 kilometers) per hour. But they can speed up to almost 20 miles (32 km) per hour to **ambush** and catch their prey.

Tiger sharks will sometimes jump out of the water when hunting.

DID YOU KNOW?

Most tiger sharks can grow up to 18 feet (5.5 meters) long. Female tiger sharks are bigger than males.

CHAPTER THREE

How are tiger shark babies born?

DID YOU KNOW?
Baby sharks are called pups.

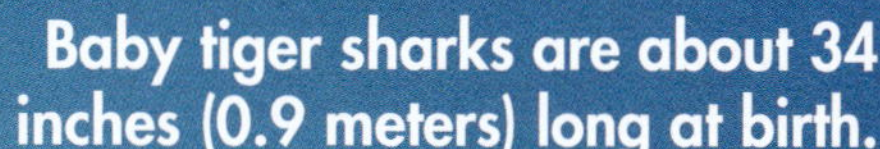

Baby tiger sharks are about 34 inches (0.9 meters) long at birth.

The babies grow inside their mother for up to 16 months. They are born in groups of 10 to 82 babies. Their mothers do not help them find food or take care of them. The babies are left on their own.

Do tiger sharks swim together?

Not usually. Tiger sharks are **solitary** animals. They swim alone. They hunt alone. Tiger sharks only come together to **breed** in the spring. They also sometimes swim in groups when eating large animals together.

A tiger shark will swim with another before mating.

Are tiger sharks endangered?

No, but the population is decreasing. **Overfishing** is the biggest threat to tiger sharks. Many people use the sharks' fins in soup. Their skin is used as leather. Some people also kill them out of fear.

It is against the law to catch a tiger shark in Australia and Florida, USA.

ASK MORE QUESTIONS

Do tiger sharks stay in one place?

How long do tiger sharks live?

Try a BIG QUESTION: How can humans help tiger sharks?

SEARCH FOR ANSWERS

Search the library catalog or the Internet.
A librarian, teacher, or parent can help you.

Using Keywords
Find the looking glass.

Keywords are the most important words in your question.

If you want to know about:

- whether tiger sharks move, type: TIGER SHARK MIGRATION
- how long a tiger shark lives, type: TIGER SHARK LIFESPAN

FIND GOOD SOURCES

Some are better than others. An adult can help you look. Here are some good, safe sources.

Books

Tiger Sharks
by Marysa Storm, 2024.

Tiger Shark
by Rachel Rose, 2022.

Internet Sites

Animal Corner | Tiger Shark
https://animalcorner.org/animals/tiger-shark/
Learn more information about tiger sharks.

Britannica Kids | Tiger Shark
https://kids.britannica.com/kids/article/tiger-shark/639071
Britannica has fact-checked articles about many different topics.

Every effort has been made to ensure that these websites are appropriate for children. However, because of the nature of the Internet, it is impossible to guarantee that these sites will remain active indefinitely or that their contents will not be altered.

SHARE AND TAKE ACTION

Create a trivia game using facts about tiger sharks. Have fun playing a game and learning shark facts with your friends.

Host a shark week at your school. Share posters about tiger sharks and other cool sharks you have studied.

Plastic and other trash are bad for ocean animals. Plan a beach cleanup with your friends and family.

GLOSSARY

aggressive Showing a readiness to fight or attack.

ambush A surprise attack.

appetite A want or need to eat.

breed The process by which young animals are produced by their parents.

mate To pair up to produce young.

overfish To catch too many fish at a rate faster than they are born.

prey An animal hunted for food.

solitary Living or being alone.

INDEX

About the Author

Debra Randorf lives and works in Minneapolis, Minnesota. She is so curious, she goes to the library at least once a week.